THE MONOPOLY GAME
PRACTICE SET

ACCOUNTING FOR MONOPOLY GAME TRANSACTIONS

W. ROBERT KNECHEL

UNIVERSITY OF FLORIDA

THE DRYDEN PRESS

HARCOURT BRACE COLLEGE PUBLISHERS

FORT WORTH   PHILADELPHIA   SAN DIEGO   NEW YORK   ORLANDO   AUSTIN   SAN ANTONIO
TORONTO   MONTREAL   LONDON   SYDNEY   TOKYO

Address for Editorial Correspondence
The Dryden Press, 301 Commerce Street, Suite 3700, Fort Worth, TX 76102

Address for Orders
The Dryden Press, 6277 Sea Harbor Drive, Orlando, FL 32887
1-800-782-4479, or 1-800-433-0001 (in Florida)

ISBN: 0-15-500304-6

Printed in the United States of America

4 5 6 7 8 9 0 1   0 5 6   9 8 7 6 5 4

The Dryden Press
Harcourt Brace & Company

TO THE STUDENT

The game of *MONOPOLY*® has been popular with generations of children and adults since its first widespread publication in 1935. People around the world have spent countless hours wheeling and dealing in real estate transactions that, with a few zeros added to the numbers, would awe Donald Trump. Furthermore, the game is fraught with amazingly timely perils that can trip up the most wary player, for example, deals that go bad, bankruptcy and even jail. For a relatively simple game that is easy to learn to play, the *MONOPOLY* game offers great challenges to those who consider themselves potential real estate tycoons.

Since most people learn how to play the *MONOPOLY* game when they are children, they often fail to appreciate that the game is actually a complex business simulation, illustrating many of the factors that affect any business that is trying to develop and become successful. Players are challenged with the need to acquire assets so as to produce a future stream of revenue that will create profits for the player (or their firm). The players must consider the cost of acquiring these assets as well as their ability to manage the assets so as to produce the maximum revenue. In the game of *MONOPOLY*, the players' assets are real estate (developed and undeveloped); their costs are the acquisition price of those assets as well as incidental costs such as taxes, interest, rent and other payments; and their revenues are rents received and salary collected on passing "GO." The object of the game is to achieve revenues that exceed costs and to do this better than any of the competition, much as in the real world of business.

The purpose of this practice set is to introduce you to the inherent connection between business operations (for example, the process of attempting to earn a profit) and the accounting process which provides a record of the activities of the business enterprise. The game of *MONOPOLY* is used as a business simulation because it results in interesting and unique transactions and because the game is well known to most students.

In this practice set, you will be responsible for making the business decisions that determine the ultimate success of your enterprise as well as preparing the history of these decisions (in the form of financial statements). If you do well, your financial statements will reflect success; if you do not, your financial statements will probably look bleak. The assignments that follow require you to play the game of *MONOPOLY* and to use your accounting skills to record the events and transactions in accordance with current accounting standards . You will continually be faced with both business and accounting decisions. In this way you will see the direct connection between what you decide and how it impacts your financial statements.

iv

TO THE INSTRUCTOR

Practice sets are a common element of many financial accounting courses. The primary purpose of most traditional practice sets is to introduce the accounting and bookkeeping process that is used in business enterprises. Traditional practice sets have a number of drawbacks, however. They tend to be relatively sterile simulations of the business environment since students are given a list of transactions that have already occurred. As a result, students often fail to see the connection between actual business decisions and the financial results that follow. Students perceive accounting as a mechanical scorekeeping process that is somehow independent of the business enterprise. This is an unfortunate perception and creates a negative impression of the accounting profession.

The *MONOPOLY*® game is a relatively simple, widely available and well-known business simulation that lends itself to teaching accounting procedures. By playing the game <u>and</u> keeping detailed accounting records, students are introduced to the dynamic nature of business decisions and their connection to accounting. By adding the element of active participation in a (simulated) business environment, students are motivated to learn about accounting procedures and the preparation of financial statements.

Previous experiences have shown that students respond well to this approach to an accounting practice set.[1] Students enjoy the competitive nature of the *MONOPOLY* game and are able to view accounting as a dynamic system of record-keeping. The student instructions are clearly written and have been tested repeatedly at a number of different colleges and universities.

There are also a number of advantages to the instructor of using the *MONOPOLY* game practice set. Since the transactions that occur for each student are different, there is no single unique solution which can be copied by multiple students. Each student generates his or her own transactions and, therefore, must generate his or her own financial statements. Furthermore, the grading of the practice set is facilitated by the detailed Instructor's Manual that is provided, complete with grading guidelines and suggestions. With these guidelines, grading the *MONOPOLY* game practice set is much easier than might be initially anticipated.

The use of the *MONOPOLY* game practice set also allows the instructor a great deal of flexibility. The practice set contains numerous options for the instructor to select from and allows assignments to be varied each term. The Instructor's Manual contains eight different variations on the basic assignments which can be selected depending on the instructor's learning objectives. However, the number of additional variations that can be constructed is limited only by the instructor's imagination.

Regardless of which variation you select for your students, you can be assured that your students will find the experience of using the game of *MONOPOLY* as an accounting practice set to be both enjoyable and educational.

---

[1] For more detail see "Using a Business Simulation Game as a Substitute for a Practice Set" by W. Robert Knechel published in *Issues in Accounting Education*, Fall 1989, pp. 411-424.

ACKNOWLEDGMENTS

As with all endeavors that are worthwhile, this one could not have been completed without the support of a great number of people. Of primary importance is the support that I have received from my wife, Kimberly, and my daughter, Abigail. Both have been extremely understanding of the time demands which were necessary to complete this manuscript. Additionally, I appreciate my wife's sportsmanship in helping to pilot test an early version of the practice set.

I would like to thank Gary and Laura McGill who also assisted in the pilot testing of an early version of the practice set.

Many students have contributed their views to this effort and have helped make this a challenging and rewarding learning experience. Of most importance are the experiences of the MBA students at the University of Florida who have worked their way through the various evolutions of this practice set. I also appreciate the comments and suggestions from my colleagues around the country who have undertaken similar experiments in response to my paper published in *Issues in Accounting Education*. I would especially like to thank Richard S. Rand Jr. (Tennessee Technological University and author of the Instructor's Manual) for his assistance. Others who have communicated their support of the ideas incorporated in this practice set include Doug Snowball (University of Florida), James Frederickson (Indiana University), Ron Huefner (State University of New York at Buffalo), Ceil M. Pillsbury (University of Wisconsin—Green Bay) and Kevin D. Stocks (Brigham Young University). I appreciate receiving all comments and suggestions.

Again, I hope you find the experience of this practice set to be enjoyable and educational.

W. Robert Knechel

CONTENTS

OVERVIEW

AN INTRODUCTION TO THE GAME OF *MONOPOLY*®

The game of *MONOPOLY* is a board game that is based on the principles of buying, developing and selling real estate. Players move their game piece around a square board that has 40 spaces. Twenty-eight squares on the board represent properties that players may purchase. The properties fall into three categories: railroads (4), utilities (2) or undeveloped land (22). The objective of the game is to acquire as many properties as possible. Possession of a property allows the player to collect rent from other players whenever they land on it. In this way, acquisition of properties creates an incoming stream of revenue.

The undeveloped properties are color-coded into groups. If a player manages to obtain all the properties in a color-coded group, that player possesses a "monopoly". Once a player obtains a monopoly, he or she can begin to develop all the properties in the group by constructing houses and hotels. Such development increases the amount of rent that the owner collects when other players land on the property. Obviously, acquiring a completed monopoly is critical to success in the game. On the other hand, avoiding other players' properties is also important so as to avoid paying rent.

A number of squares on the game board do not represent properties but, instead, direct the player to perform specific activities that typically involve expending or receiving cash. Many of these activities are directed by cards that are selected from a stack. The game has two sets of cards: *Chance* and *Community Chest*. When a player selects one of these cards, he or she follows the instructions on the card and replaces the card at the bottom of the stack (it may come up again if the entire stack is used during the course of the game). Some cards provide for delayed action, in which case the player keeps the card until it is needed (and then it is replaced in the stack).

The board has four corner squares that are of special significance:

GO: This is the starting point for the game. Put all player pieces here initially. Every time a player goes completely around the board, that is, he or she returns to GO, the player is said to have "passed GO". For this, the player collects $200. Occasionally, a player is directed to jump directly to a specific square on the Board. All such movement is assumed to be in a forward direction so a player may pass GO while making such a move. The player is entitled to collect $200 (unless specifically told otherwise).

JAIL: This is the square that players go to when they are directed to "Jail". A player directed to Jail must stay there until he or she pays $50, rolls doubles, or uses a "get out of jail free" card. If a player doesn't meet the last two conditions within three turns, he or she must pay the $50. Players who land on this square directly as a result of the dice roll are not considered to be "in jail", but instead, are "just visiting". They can proceed onward on their next turn at no cost or penalty.

FREE PARKING: Nothing happens here. Players should be warned that many variations have developed over time which allow alternative uses for this square. One common variation is that a player landing on Free Parking collects a bonus. The *MONOPOLY* game rules, however, indicate that absolutely nothing happens when a player lands here. Players should follow the correct rule and not any variations that they may know.

GO TO JAIL: This space means exactly what it says (refer to the JAIL square above). Players do not pass GO when they have to go to jail so they do not collect $200. Also, certain game cards direct a player to go to jail. A third way to get to jail is if a player roll doubles three times in succession.

PLAYING THE GAME:

Players select the game piece they wish to use and place it on GO. They also get $1,500 from the bank. Players roll the dice to see who goes first. Players move their pieces in a clockwise direction around the board based on the number on the dice. That is, if a player rolls an eight, he or she moves the game piece 8 spaces (not counting the one they are currently on). The player will perform any action that is appropriate for the square that he or she lands on. If a player rolls doubles, he or she gets to go again. However, if a player rolls doubles a third time, the player must go directly to Jail.

A single "turn" is completed when every player who is entitled to has had an opportunity to roll the dice and move . Note that some players may move more than once (due to rolling doubles) or may not move at all (being in jail or having been directed to lose a turn). In any event, a single complete turn represents one cycle of play. You will be playing the game for the number of turns specified by your instructor.

AN INTRODUCTION TO THE TRANSACTIONS OF THE GAME OF *MONOPOLY*

A vast array of transactions can occur during any game of *MONOPOLY*. Players must be continually aware of transactions that may have an impact on the financial status of their own company, even if the transaction occurs during another player's "turn". These transactions should be "recorded" as part of the accounting records (see Assignment I). Some of the common transactions are summarized below:

1. Initial capitalization: Each player receives $1,500 in cash from the bank. This represents the initial capitalization for each player. This transaction should be recorded by each player as:

Cash	1,500	
Contributed Capital		1,500

2. Buying property, houses and hotels from the bank: Players may purchase properties after landing on one that is unowned. Players may also purchase houses and hotels at any time after they have completed a color-group monopoly.

> Example: Player A lands on and buys "Boardwalk" for $400. Player A would prepare the following entry:

A: Land (Boardwalk)	400	
Cash		400

3. Paying and receiving rent: When one player lands on a property owned by another, rent must be paid to the owner. The amount of the rent will depend on the property and whether it contains houses or a hotel.

> Example: Player B lands on "Boardwalk" which is owned by Player A. B pays $50 to A. Players A and B prepare the following entries, respectively:

A: Cash	50	
Rent Revenue		50
B: Rent Expense	50	
Cash		50

4. Passing "Go" and collecting salary from the bank: Players should consider this to be for consulting services.

> Example: Player A passes "Go" and collects $200

A: Cash	200	
Consulting Revenue		200

5. Paying or receiving cash as a result of *Chance* or *Community Chest* cards: These cards direct the player to perform specific actions. Some of the possibilities are:

> a. Advance to a specific square and purchase a property or pay rent (see 2 and 3 above).

> b. Receive money. This cash flow should be recorded and classified as accurately as possible.

> c. Pay fees, taxes or fines. This cash flow should be recorded and classified as accurately as possible.

> d. Go to Jail.

> e. Get Out of Jail Free. This is self-explanatory but players may wish to discuss what (if any) accounting recognition is appropriate for this event.

f. Pay assessments on properties. The total amount to be paid by the player being assessed depends on all the property he or she has at that time. Players may wish to discuss whether this should be capitalizable cost or should be expensed.

[NOTE: Assignment I describes some alternative interpretations for the *Chance* and *Community Chest* cards that your instructor may ask you to use in order to increase the business and accounting realism of the practice set.]

6. Mortgaging properties: The game allows a player to borrow money against the value of an undeveloped property. The maximum amount that can be borrowed is 50% of the nominal property value. Note, mortgaging a property precludes the collection of rent on that property. The mortgage may be paid off at any time by paying back the borrowed amount plus 10% (regardless of how long the mortgage is outstanding).

7. Selling or trading properties to other players: Players may decide to buy, sell or trade properties among each other. This is allowed and may be the best way for players to complete monopolies. The accounting for these transactions can be complicated, however, and players should carefully discuss the possibilities at the time the transaction occurs. Be sure to provide a full explanation for these transactions when making an entry in the accounting records. A significant issue that must be resolved is the "cost" to be assigned to a property that has been acquired in a swap. Should the cost of the new property be equal to the cost of the old property, its nominal cost, or something else? Students should refer to the discussion of nonmonetary exchanges (of similar assets) in their accounting text for further detail.

8. Selling houses or hotels to bank: Previously acquired houses or hotels may need to be sold back to the bank in order to fulfill a player's obligations. Houses and hotels may not be sold to other players under any circumstances. Unfortunately, the bank only pays 50% of the original cost. This will necessitate recognition of a loss by the player. Be sure to consider any capitalized costs (in addition to the original acquisition cost) which may affect the size of the loss to be recorded.

[NOTE: Players do not need to record depreciation on houses or hotels that have been sold. Recognition of part-year depreciation expense would simply reduce the amount of the loss recorded on the sale. Therefore, net income is not affected by the failure to record depreciation. This is a common practice in real accounting systems since it is simpler and does not distort reported results.]

9. Forgiving rent or accepting other consideration in lieu of rent: There may arise situations where one player will reduce or forgive rent owed by another player in exchange for some other consideration, typically, transfer of a property from the owing player to the collecting player. This transaction is similar to selling or trading properties (see 7 above) and players must consider many of the same accounting issues. A key accounting issue is the amount of rent expense/revenue that should be recorded. Should the expense/revenue be equal to the stated rent or some other value since the stated rent was not paid in cash?

10. Paying income taxes: One of the squares on the game board requires a player to pay income taxes. The player has the choice of paying $200 or 10% of their <u>total</u> assets (including cash on hand and the value of all property). Certain game cards also direct that a player is to receive an income tax refund. Players should consider these transactions in anticipation of final settlement of the income tax liability at the end of the game (to be based on a player's actual results). Therefore, taxes paid during the game should be considered "prepaid" and tax refunds received should be netted against any prepaid amounts. All players will compute and record their actual tax expense for the period of the game when the game is over (see Assignment II). Note, other taxes that a player may pay should be considered an expense as incurred and do not affect income taxes.

WARNING: Most recordable transactions will occur during a player's own turn. But, collecting rent and some other actions may occur during another player's turn. **Don't forget to consider the accounting ramifications of <u>all</u> transactions!**

THE ASSIGNMENTS:

The next section begins the actual assignments for this practice set. There are four possible assignments, each of which has multiple parts. Your instructor will provide you with further information about completing the assignments. You should refer to Table O-1, which lists a number of options available to the instructor. The instructor will provide you with a completed version of this form or will provide you the appropriate information in class. **Be careful to note the exact choices that your instructor has made in order to ensure that you complete the practice set appropriately.**

Good luck and have fun! May the best person win!

TABLE O-1

SUMMARY OF GAME OPTIONS

INSTRUCTOR NAME: _____

Your instructor will provide you with the following information:

(1) Number of game turns: _____

(2) Requirements to Complete (Check all that apply):

Assignment I	Assignment II	Assignment III	Assignment IV
Requirement (1) ___	Requirement (1) ___	Requirement (1) ___	Requirement (1) ___
Requirement (2) ___	Requirement (2) ___	Requirement (2) ___	Requirement (2) ___
Requirement (3) ___	Requirement (3) ___	Requirement (3) ___	Requirement (3) ___
	Requirement (4) ___		Requirement (4) ___
	Requirement (5) ___		Requirement (5) ___
	Requirement (6) ___		Requirement (6) ___
	Requirement (7) ___		

(3) Journals, Ledgers and Workpapers to use (Check all that apply):

General Journal _____
General Ledger _____
Cash Receipts Journal _____
Cash Disbursements Journal _____
Long-term Assets Ledger _____ (See Tables I-3 and I-4)
Notes Payable Ledger _____ (See Table I-3)
Adjusting Entry Worksheet _____

(4) Game Cards to Use for *Chance* and *Community Chest* (Check ONE only):

Standard Monopoly Cards ____
Alternative Interpretations of Standard Cards ____ (See Table I-1)
Substitute Card Selection Procedure ____ (See Appendix to Assign. I)

(5) Instructor Selected Optional Rules to Use (Check all that apply, See Table I-2):

OR1   Appraised value of real estate ____
OR2   Avoiding bankruptcy ____
OR3   Auctioning all property ____
OR4   Mortgaged properties ____
OR5   Interest costs ____

(6) Depreciation Method: _____   Part Year Depreciation: _____

ASSIGNMENT I

THE RECOGNITION AND MEASUREMENT PROCESS

The first step in the accounting process is to identify transactions that should be recorded in the financial records of an enterprise. Decisions made, events that occur and conditions that change may all result in consequences that should be reflected in the financial records. Accountants use the term **recordable events** to refer to these consequences.

Once a recordable event has been identified, the accountant must assign a numerical value (in terms of dollars) to what has happened. In most cases, the assignation of a dollar value to a transaction is relatively easy because an observable **exchange price** has been agreed upon by two parties. In other cases, assigning a value may be difficult, especially when conditions change without any specific action on the part of the company. An example of this type of difficulty occurs when property values for real estate decline due to general market conditions. An accountant may realize that an asset has lost value but will be unable to determine a reasonable value to place on the loss.

The remainder of this section describes the practice set and your first set of assignments.

GETTING STARTED:

Your instructor will divide the class into groups for playing the game of *MONOPOLY*®. You will probably have a total of four or five players in your group (counting yourself). **Each player in the group represents a separate company**.

Each group should agree as to when they will get together to actually play the game. Your instructor will tell you how many turns you will need to play in the game (52 turns is typical since each turn then represents a week). You should plan on setting aside at least three hours to actually play the game. You will need additional time to complete any additional assignments that the instructor requires but they can usually be completed on your own time, outside your group.

You will need a copy of the game when the group gets together to play. If you don't already have a copy, the game of *MONOPOLY* is available in most toy stores. Alternatively, your instructor may be able to provide you with a copy of the game.

When your group first meets, you should review the rules of the game. For this exercise, standard *MONOPOLY* game rules will be used. Variations are not allowed (for example, there is no reward for landing on "Free Parking" and all fines and penalties are paid to the bank). Do not use the rules for the short game. You should also review the options chosen by your instructor and summarized in Table O-1.

Players must also agree as to who will be the "banker". Being banker does not involve any additional accounting effort and does not affect the process of recognizing transactions that occur for that player. The banker, however, should be someone who is familiar with the rules of the game since they must often perform some action when other players have transactions (for example, money for purchasing property goes into the bank and should be counted and verified by the banker).

Finally, the players need to identify which approach they will use for *Chance* and *Community Chest* spaces on the board. Your instructor will tell you which of the following three options you are to use (see Table O-1):

1. *MONOPOLY* Game Cards: Use the cards that are included in the game. No modifications are made to how the *Chance* or *Community Chest* cards are interpreted.

2. Alternative Interpretations of *MONOPOLY* Game Cards: Use the cards that are included in the game but check Table I-1 for alternative interpretations for some of the cards. If the card appears in Table I-1, then you should ignore what the card says and follow the alternative instructions listed in the table.

3. Substitute Card Selection Procedure: Ignore the cards that are included in the game and instead roll one die and then the other to identify which of 36 substitute "cards" should be used. Full instructions for this option appear on page 20.

Regardless of the approach that is used, the cards are the source of some of the most interesting events that occur in the game and create some interesting accounting problems. The members of each group should discuss the accounting issues related to these cards whenever one is selected by any player.

TO START PLAY:

Give each player $1,500 in cash from the bank. This represents the initial and only source of equity capital for each player. Determine which player is to go first and follow the standard rules for the game of MONOPOLY. A complete turn occurs after each player has had a chance to move once.

INSTRUCTOR SELECTED OPTIONAL RULES:

Table I-2 contains some optional rules that your instructor may decide to invoke. Your instructor's choices should be listed in Table O-1. **You should only use these rules when your instructor specifically tells you to!**

REQUIREMENTS:

1. Set up your accounting system:

The Working Papers section of the practice set contains numerous blank forms and schedules that you will need in order to set up the accounting system for the real estate company that you will be managing. In some cases, column headings have been entered for you so as to help you understand the use of each schedule. Extra blank schedules are also provided in case you fill up any of the pre-formatted schedules. The pages that you may need for completing Assignment I are:

(a) **General Journal**: Used to record all transactions that do not get recorded in the specialized journals.
(b) **Specialized Journal for Cash Receipts**: Used to record all transactions involving the receipt of cash.
(c) **Specialized Journal for Cash Disbursements**: Used to record all transactions involving the expenditure of cash.
(d) **Long-term Assets Ledger**: Used to list all properties that are owned by a player, including pertinent data that will be needed to complete future assignments.
(e) **Notes Payable Ledger**: Used to list all loans obtained from the bank by a player, including pertinent data that will be needed to complete future assignments.

Players should familiarize themselves with the format and use of these schedules before they start the game. Your instructor may indicate that you are to use only some of these schedules (see Table O-1).

2. Journalize transactions as they occur.

Play the game and prepare journal entries for all events and transactions that affect your financial status. You should make each entry in the appropriate journal (that is, the General Journal or a Specialized Journal) given the nature of the transaction.

Journal entries should be "dated" by week (rather than by turn). For example, a transaction occurring in the first turn will be dated as 1/93 (week 1, 1993) and a transaction occurring in turn 52 will be dated as 52/93 (week 52, 1993). The dates are very important for completing future assignments. Full explanations should be provided, especially for unusual transactions. Don't forget that you may need to record some events that occur during another player's turn.

Be careful to record all of your transactions. Do not wait until the end of the game to prepare your journal entries. Failure to record a transaction will probably result in a discrepancy between the amount of cash you actually have on hand versus the amount that the general ledger will show after posting (see Assignment II). If you are unsure of how to account for a transaction, discuss the proper treatment with other players in your game.

3. Maintain the Long-term Assets Ledger and Notes Payable Ledger.

In addition to preparing standard journal entries, you should also keep the Long-term Assets Ledger (LAL) and the Notes Payable Ledger (NPL) up to date. The column headings in these ledgers are self-explanatory. Whenever you purchase a property, add it the LAL. Whenever you dispose of a property, enter the pertinent information in the LAL. When you borrow money from the Bank, enter the data in the NPL. When you pay it back, also note the data in the NPL. This information will be helpful to you when you go to complete Assignment II. [NOTE: See Tables I-3 and I-4 for more information on how to use the Long-term Assets and Notes Payable Ledgers.]

TABLE I-1

ALTERNATIVE INTERPRETATIONS FOR
CHANCE AND *COMMUNITY CHEST* CARDS

CHANCE CARD

You have been elected Chairman of the Board. Pay each player $50.

Your building and loan matures. Collect $150.

Pay poor tax of $15.

NEW INTERPRETATION

You have lost an antitrust lawsuit. Pay $50 to each player.

Obtain rent advance of $150. The rental period is 25 turns starting with the current turn.

Pay $15 for termite inspection of properties.

COMMUNITY CHEST CARD

Pay hospital $100.

You inherit $100.

Doctor's fee. Pay $50.

You have won second prize in a beauty contest. Collect $10.

Receive $25 for services.

Life insurance matures. Collect $100.

Grand opera opening. Collect $50 from every player.

Xmas fund matures. Collect $100.

From sale of stock, you get $45.

NEW INTERPRETATION

Pay $104 for health insurance on employees. Coverage is for 52 turns starting with current turn.

You receive $100 government grant to improve properties.

Pay your attorney $50 for work on lawsuits.

You win $10 award for beautification of property.

Issue common stock for $25.

Collect $100 from insurance company for repairs to property.

You have won an anti-trust lawsuit against your competitors. Collect $50 from each player.

Obtain rent advance of $100. The rental period is 25 turns starting with current turn.

Issue common stock for $45.

TABLE I-2

INSTRUCTOR SELECTED OPTIONAL RULES

OR1. Appraised value of real estate:

Rules: The *MONOPOLY* game contains no mechanism for determining the fair market value of property as anything other than the nominal value listed on the game board.

Optional Rule: Assume that the market value of all real estate is equal to the nominal value indicated on the game board. Effective at the beginning of Turn 25, the values should be increased by 10%, e.g., Boardwalk rises in value to $440 which becomes its purchase price if it has not yet been acquired by any player. This rule will have an impact on the accounting for some transactions, specifically when players swap property. Rental and mortgage values are not affected by this change.

OR2. Avoiding bankruptcy:

Rule: When a player runs out of cash and property and still owes money to a player or the bank, that player is considered bankrupt and would be out of the game. Financial statements could be prepared as of the date of bankruptcy but would show little of interest.

Optional Rule: Assume that no player is allowed to go "bankrupt". If a player runs out of cash and has no remaining property (and, thus, would normally be out of the game), the bank will advance the player as much money (in multiples of $200) as he or she needs to keep in the game. For example, assume Player A owes $350 to Player B for rent but only has $75 on hand. The bank will lend $400 to A to use to pay B (leaving A with $125). This loan is unsecured since the player has no remaining property to use as collateral. These loans carry an interest rate of 15% (they are very high risk).

OR3. Auctioning all property:

Rule: When a player lands on a property, he or she has the right of first refusal to acquire that property. If the player decides to acquire the property, then he or she pays the nominal value to the bank and takes possession. If the player chooses not to acquire the property, then it is auctioned off to the highest bidder among the players.

Optional Rule: A property is put up for auction when any player lands on it. That is, there is no right of first refusal for the moving player and all property is to be auctioned regardless of who lands it. Rental and mortgage values are not affected by this change.

TABLE I-2 (Continued)

OR4. Mortgaged properties:

Rule: Only undeveloped properties may be mortgaged. Players may <u>not</u> collect rent on undeveloped properties that have been mortgaged (which by definition do not contain houses).

Optional Rule: Players may mortgage any property, including those with houses (although the presence of houses or a hotel does not change the amount that can be borrowed). Also, players may collect 50% of the normal rental value during the period that a property is mortgaged.

OR5. Interest Costs:

Rule: The bank charges 10% for all borrowed funds (i.e., mortgages) regardless of how long the mortgage is outstanding.

Optional Rule. The bank charges interest at the rate of 0.25% per turn (rounded up to the nearest dollar). For example, if Player A borrows $100 on Turn 16 and repays it on Turn 30, Player A would owe interest of $4 ($100 x 14 turns x .0025 = $3.50, rounded to $4). [This rule is interesting and more realistic when combined with OR4].

TABLE I-3

USE OF LONG-TERM ASSETS AND NOTES PAYABLE LEDGERS

Notes Payable Ledger (NPL)

Column 1   Enter the identity of the property that has been mortgaged.

Column 2   Enter the date that the money was borrowed from the bank.

Column 3   Enter the amount of money that has been borrowed. This will usually be 50% of the nominal property value.

Column 4   If the loan has been repaid, enter the date of repayment.

Column 5   Enter the total amount of the repayment including interest.

Column 6   Enter the amount of interest paid. Interest is 10% of the borrowed amount, regardless of how long the loan is outstanding (unless you are using Optional Rule OR5).

Column 7   Enter the amount of year-end interest accrual. This is described in more detail in Assignment II and would not be done until the end of the game.

NOTE: Table I-3 continues on the next page with the Long-term Assets Ledger.

TABLE I-3 (Continued)

Long-term Assets Ledger (LAL)

Column 1   Asset Description: Enter the identity of the property or asset. This will usually be the name of the property, for example, "Boardwalk".

Column 2:   Type of Asset: Indicate if the asset is land, house, hotel or other (for example, capital improvements to houses). All assets except land are depreciated Players should use a separate line for each property and for each house, hotel or improvement to that property. One suggestion is to leave 7 blank lines between each piece of land entered in the ledger. This will provide space immediately after the land to enter other assets related to that land, such as houses.

Column 3   Enter the date the asset was acquired, that is, the turn.

Column 4   Enter the acquisition price of the asset.

Column 5   Enter the expected useful life of the asset. For houses this is 8 years, for hotels it is 15 years (unless your instructor indicates otherwise).

Column 6   Annual depreciation expense: This should be computed using the method stipulated by your instructor (straight line, declining balance or sum-of-the-year's digits). This column would only be filled in at the end of the game. See Table O-1 for the depreciation method to use.

Column 7   Current year depreciation should be computed by prorating the amount in Column 6 over the portion of the current year that you possess the asset. Alternatively, your instructor may indicate to use a half-year convention for the year an asset is acquired. This column would only be filled in at the end of the game. See Table O-1 for the method of proration to use.

Column 8   If the asset has been sold, enter the date of sale.

Column 9   If the asset has been sold, enter the selling price.

Column 10   If the asset has been sold, compute the gain.

NOTE: Players do not need to compute depreciation on assets that have been sold. This results in an understatement of depreciation expense for that asset. The understatement is offset by recognition of a smaller gain (or larger loss) when the sale of the asset is recorded. As a practical matter, this approach is simpler to use and has no net impact on net income.

TABLE I-4

EXAMPLE: USE OF THE LONG-TERM ASSETS LEDGER (LAL)

Long-Term Assets Ledger

Asset Description	Type? Land/ House	Date (Turn) Bought	Price Paid	Exp. Life	Annual Deprctn. Expense	Deprctn. Expense: Current	Date (Turn) Sold	Selling Price	Gain or (Loss)
Park Place	Land	5	350	—	—	—			
House 1	House	17	200	8	25	17			
House 2	House	22	200	8	25	14			
Boardwalk	Land	16	400	—	—	—			
House 1	House	17	200	8	25	17			
House 2	House	22	200	8	25	14			
House 3	House	29	200	8	25	—	40	100	(100)
Baltic Avenue	Land	22	60	—	—	—	42	130	70

APPENDIX TO ASSIGNMENT I

PROCEDURE FOR USE OF SUBSTITUTE CARD SELECTION

When using the substitution procedure described below, you will leave the *Chance* and *Community Chest* cards in the game box. Do not place the cards on the game board, as you will not be using them.

Instead, when you land on a *Chance* or *Community Chest* space, you will roll each die, one at a time, to find the appropriate set of instructions to use from the next three pages. The first die you roll will indicate the column to select and the second roll will indicate the row to select. **The dice should be rolled one at a time, not together.**

For example, say you land on *Chance*. Your first die roll is a three so you go to the column marked with the face of a die showing three dots (columns are marked by the die faces at the <u>top</u>). With your second die you roll a four so you move down the column to the fourth row, marked with a die face showing four dots (rows are marked by the die faces to the <u>side</u>). Column three, row four provides the following instructions:

> " A movie company wants to use one of your
> properties as a set. Collect $200."

You would then execute these instructions just as you would with a regular *Chance* card.

Advance to the nearest color-coded property you own. This property is to be condemned by the government. Collect $250 from the bank and turn over the deed. No player may ever repurchase this property.	Advance to the nearest color-coded property you own. Your employees go on strike for the next four turns at this location. Collect no rent during that time.
Advance to the nearest color-coded property you own. This property has been found in violation of building codes. Pay $150 to make capital improvements.	A local ordnance is passed mandating handicap access to all houses and hotels. Pay $30 per house and $100 per hotel to make capital improvements to your properties.
Bank pays you interest on your account. Collect an amount equal to 10% of your cash on hand (rounded down to the nearest dollar).	You decide to run for election. Pay $25 for the cost of your campaign. Also, you may not collect rents during the next turn. (Sorry, you lose the election.)
Business demands require that you advance to Boardwalk. You may purchase the property if it unowned. If it is already owned by another player, pay the normal rent.	You decide to take the next two weeks off. Go directly to GO and collect $400. You lose your next two turns, however. (You may still collect rent on your properties.)
Bank pays you interest on your account. Collect an amount equal to 10% of your cash on hand (rounded down to the nearest dollar).	You decide to take next week off. Go directly to GO and collect $200. You lose your next turn, however. (You may still collect rent on your properties.)
Advance to the nearest color-coded property you own. Toxic wastes have been discovered beneath the surface. Pay $250 to clean up the waste. Also pay $50 to the owner(s) of the two immediately adjacent properties (i.e., one on either side) to settle related lawsuits.	Advance to the nearest color-coded property you own. A new school is to be built nearby which will increase your property value. Double the rental value of this property for the remainder of the game. (Make a note of this so you don't forget!)

You are considering investing in railroads. Advance to the nearest railroad that is unowned. You may purchase the railroad at a $50 discount if it is unowned. If owned by another player, however, pay double the normal rent.	The manager of one of your properties absconds with the rent money. The very next player who lands on one of your properties pays the rent money to the bank (not you). After that, you may collect rent as usual.
You are considering investing in a utility. Advance to the nearest utility that is unowned. You may purchase the utility at a $30 discount if it is unowned. If owned by another player, however, pay rent of $50 (rather than the normal rent).	You are declared Person-of-the-Week by the local Better Business Bureau. All players (except you) must pay $25 to the bank to attend your testimonial dinner.
Advance to the nearest property that you own. This location is discovered to have historical significance. The rental value for this property is increased $20 for the remainder of the game. (Make a note of this so you don't forget!)	One of your properties is selected as the "Best Landscaped" in the area. Collect a prize of $50.
A movie company wants to use one of your properties as a set. Collect $200.	Receive $200 for consulting services provided to real estate developers in another state.
You are convicted of illegal dumping of building materials and other garbage. GO TO JAIL. DO NOT PASS GO AND DO NOT COLLECT $200.	GET OUT OF JAIL FREE (But pay your attorney $10)
The NCAA basketball championships are being held near your properties next week. Due to the resulting demand for rooms, you are able to raise the rents on _all_ your properties by $20 for the next _two_ turns.	Pay a professional licensing tax of $15.

Advance to the nearest color-coded property you own. A mobile home park opens nearby and reduces the value of that property. Decrease the rental value of this property by 50% for the remainder of the game. (Make a note of this so you don't forget!)	Win lawsuit against the contractor who built your houses and hotels. Collect $20 per house and $70 per hotel on your properties at this time.
Receive HUD grant to subsidize building cost in low income areas. You may build <u>one</u> house on any Monopoly you own at 50% of the normal cost. This card may be saved for use in a future turn or may be sold to another player.	Advance to the nearest color-coded property that you own that does not have a hotel. The City would like to rent this property on a long term basis. <u>If you wish</u>, collect $500 plus $150 for each house on the property. If you take the money now, all players land here rent free in the future.
Advance to the nearest <u>undeveloped</u> property owned by another player. Pay 20 weeks worth of rent to the owner. The owner may collect rent from other players who land on the property in future turns.	Advance to the nearest color-coded property that you own. It has been found in violation of OSHA regulations. To remedy the problems, pay $30 plus (1) $10 for each house on the property <u>or</u> (2) $50 for a hotel.
Receive income tax refund of $40.	Pay $75 for health insurance for your employees. This policy provides coverage for 52 turns.
Tenant slips and falls down the steps at one of your properties. Pay $110 to settle the case out of court.	You are convicted of trying to bribe local zoning officials in order to build houses without a monopoly. GO TO JAIL (DO NOT PASS GO AND DO NOT COLLECT $200).
  GET OUT OF JAIL FREE (But pay your attorney $20)	You are assessed for street repairs. Pay $20 per house and $80 per hotel.

ASSIGNMENT II

THE POSTING PROCESS AND PREPARATION OF FINANCIAL STATEMENTS

The journal entries that you prepared as the game progressed represent a chronological history of your company. They indicate everything that has happened to the company during the course of the game, as defined by current accounting standards. This chronological history is interesting but does not provide much of an overview of the company or its performance. In order to prepare such an overview, it is necessary to summarize all of the information in the journals in a concise and easily understood manner.

The summarization of information is facilitated by the **posting process** and results, ultimately, in the preparation of financial statements. The posting process is a mechanical process whereby the information included in the chronological journals (general or specialized) is transferred to the **General Ledger** which organizes the information by category (that is, account). Most companies also use **Subsidiary Ledgers** to list specific assets or liabilities that occur in large volume. Typically, subsidiary ledgers are used for receivables and liabilities. For the game of *MONOPOLY*®, subsidiary ledgers are useful for keeping track of property and notes payable.

After completion of posting, an accountant may prepare a **Trial Balance** which lists all accounts classified as debits or credits. This is a technique to ensure that all postings have been done correctly by comparing the total debits and total credits that are recorded in the General Ledger.

Once the transactions have been posted to the General Ledger, a second process must be performed. This process is referred to as the **adjusting process** and involves modifying the accounts for any information or conditions that have not yet been acknowledged in the accounting records. Accounting standards identify many situations where accounts must be adjusted at the end of period. The cost of assets must be allocated to the periods in which they are used (depreciation), liabilities must be accrued (interest) and revenues and expenses must be adjusted so as to match the period in which they are appropriately recognized (prepaid rent expense and unearned rent revenue which pertain to future periods). In general, these adjustments fall into one of four broad categories:

   a. Expenses that have been incurred but not recognized (for example, asset costs which were capitalized and should now be written off; expenses that have not been accrued).

   b. Recorded expenses that have not yet been incurred (for example, the cost should be capitalized).

      c. Revenues that have been earned but not recognized (for example, deferred revenue that is now earned or earned revenue not yet accrued).

      d. Recorded revenue that has not yet been earned (that is, should be deferred).

At the end of each period, the accountant must go through the records and identify any situations that fall into these four categories and prepare appropriate adjusting entries. After the adjusting entries have been prepared and posted to the General Ledger, the accountant can prepare an **Adjusted Trial Balance**

The Adjusted Trial Balance serves the purpose of identifying all the accounts and their balances that should be included in the **Balance Sheet** and **Income Statement**. These statements are readily prepared using the information in the Adjusted Trial Balance. Accounts that are defined as **permanent** are included in the Balance Sheet (or Statement of Position). Accounts that are defined as **nominal** or **temporary** are included in the Income Statement.

As the last step, after the financial statements are prepared, nominal accounts must be **closed**. This means that the nominal accounts are returned to a zero balance so that they can be used to keep a record of the events of the next period. The closing process has the effect of transferring the data in the nominal accounts to a permanent account (typically, Retained Earnings). A post-closing trial balance can also be prepared which lists only the permanent accounts.

ENDING THE GAME

After your group has completed the 52 turns which comprise the game (or the number of turns specified by your instructor), you will be ready to begin Assignment II.

At the end of the last player's turn you should note your position on the game board (the space your playing piece occupies). You should also immediately count the cash that you have on hand and note the total. Finally, you should prepare a list of properties that you own at the end of the game and compare that list to the Long-term Assets Ledger you have been maintaining. Also, note if any of those properties have been mortgaged and are listed in the Notes Payable Ledger.

REQUIREMENTS:

1. Post all transactions to the General Ledger. *(P. 53)* for Each Acct Used

2. Prepare a Trial Balance.

3. Reconcile the cash on hand with the balance of the cash account.

> Any discrepancy in the cash account is probably due to the failure to record a transaction during the game. If the amounts do not agree, attempt to discover the cause of the discrepancy by comparing notes with other players. If the discrepancy can not be explained, adjust the cash balance to agree with the cash on hand. Players should not be overly concerned if this condition occurs, as long as the amounts involved are small. In real businesses such as retail stores, it is not uncommon to have a cash shortage or overage. Accountants refer to this as **Cash Over and Short**. Keep in mind, however, that the amount of cash you have is what is in your possession, not what the ledger may indicate!

4. Prepare and post year-end adjusting entries.

> The adjusting entries that are needed by any specific player will be dictated by his or her experiences during the game. You should consider whether you need to prepare any or all of the following entries. Where necessary, specific assumptions and/or options have been indicated to help you with the process.

> GENERAL ADJUSTING ENTRIES REQUIRED FOR ALL PLAYERS:

> No ↓

> a. Depreciation expense: Assume that all houses have a useful life of 8 years and all hotels have a useful life of 15 years. Depreciation should be computed based on the number of weeks that a house or hotel is owned. Undeveloped land is not depreciated. 800

> b. Consulting fee revenue: Accrue unpaid consulting fees based on the final location on the board. Accrue 1/4 of your fee for every full side of the board that you are past GO. For example, if you are on the side of the board just past GO, accrue no fee but if you are on the side with Boardwalk, accrue 75% ($150).

> c. Interest payable: If any properties are mortgaged, accrue interest at 10% for the number of weeks that the money has been borrowed. For example, if $200 was borrowed in week 20, accrue $200 x 10% x 32/52 or $12.

> d. Property taxes payable: Assume that all properties are assessed at 80% of their original cost (as indicated on the game board). Accrue tax liability equal to 5% of assessed value for all properties plus $8 for each house and $30 for each hotel on the property.

(other Payable 330)
+ Prop Tax Exp.

✗ Income taxes payable and Income tax expense: Accrue income tax expense equal to 40% of net income as reported on the income statement. Remember, you may have already paid some taxes or received refunds during the game.

OTHER ADJUSTMENTS THAT MAY BE NEEDED:

f. Depreciate capital improvements that have been mandated by the game cards (standard, alternative or substitute). Assume the useful life of the improvements is the same as the related structure (8 years for houses, 15 years for hotels).

g. Amortize health insurance premiums (alternative and substitute game cards).

h. Recognize unearned rent (alternative and substitute game cards).
MOVE FROM Asset to Exp.

5. Prepare closing entries.

6. Prepare (in good form) an Income Statement and Balance Sheet.

7. Prepare a post-closing trial balance.

NOTE: Preparation of an adjusting entry worksheet is optional (a 10-column worksheet has been included in the package if you wish to do so).

NOTE: A player who goes bankrupt should complete the assignment as of the turn that they are out of the game unless they are using the optional rule which allows players to avoid bankruptcy (OR2). Obviously, a bankrupt player will not have much of a Balance Sheet.

ASSIGNMENT III

CASH FLOW ANALYSIS

AN OVERVIEW OF CASH FLOW ANALYSIS

In Assignment II you were asked to prepare an Income Statement and Balance Sheet for your company. These statements were prepared based on accrual accounting. As such, these statements represent your best guess as to the economic effect of past events and transactions. One of the underlying principles of accrual accounting is that the effect of transactions should be spread across periods that are affected by them. Thus, we see accountants depreciating fixed assets, amortizing prepaid insurance and deferring revenue that has not been earned.

Accrual accounting information is but one way to assess the status and performance of an enterprise. An alternative approach is based on an analysis of the cash flows of an organization. Many users of financial statements like to see cash flow data because it helps them to: "(a) assess the enterprise's ability to generate positive cash flows; (b) assess the enterprise's ability to meet its obligations ...; (c) assess the reasons for differences between net income and associated cash receipts and payments; and (d) assess the effects ... of both its cash and noncash investing and financing transactions [FASB Statement 95, paragraph 5]." The Financial Accounting Standards Board has adopted the position that a Statement of Cash Flows is the best mechanism to provide this data to readers of financial statements.

FASB Statement No. 95 defines three categories of cash flows, each of which should be separately presented in the Statement of Cash Flows.

> (1) Operating Activity: This category of cash flows pertains to the day to day operations of the company. In a retail company, the activities grouped into this category include acquiring and selling merchandise along with the related costs of doing business. In the game of *MONOPOLY*®, the primary activity that would be considered to be operating is the receipt and payment of rent along with related fees, taxes, etc. Consulting revenue could also be considered to be from operations. FASB Statement No. 95 allows Cash Flows from Operations to be computed using either the Direct Method or the Indirect Method. See your accounting textbook for more detail on the two methods.

> (2) Investing Activity: This category is defined to include the cash flows associated with acquiring capital assets and other investments. Possession and use of these assets can be expected to eventually result in operating cash flows. Cash flows from disposal of these assets are also considered to be investing activity. In the game of *MONOPOLY*, the acquisition and disposal of properties and related improvements is the primary source of investing cash flows.

(3) Financing Activity: This category reflects the process of obtaining debt and equity capital for use by the enterprise. Included in this activity is the borrowing and repaying of money, the sale of stock and payments to shareholders. In the game of *MONOPOLY*, the primary source of capital is the initial capitalization. Players may also borrow money from the bank in the form of mortgages.

An effective method for analyzing cash flows is to examine individual transactions for their impact on cash flows. For example, when a player purchases a property, he or she pays cash which is a transaction that should be included in the Statement of Cash Flows as an investing activity. Similarly, all the rent that the player collects from owning the property should be reflected in the Statement as an inflow from operating activity. On the other hand, rent paid to other players or fees paid to the bank, may represent cash outflows related to operating activity.

Some recorded events or transactions may not have a cash flow impact. Most adjusting entries that are prepared at the end a period have this characteristic. When a company records depreciation, it is not reducing its cash balance. As a result, net income (after deducting depreciation) will be different from Cash Flows from Operating Activity. Other differences will also arise due to other adjusting entries.

Independent of adjusting entries, some transactions may not require the expenditure or receipt of cash, or may only have a small cash component. A common example that occurs in the game of *MONOPOLY* is when two players swap properties. If Player A swaps Boardwalk to Player B for the Reading Railroad plus $200, the only cash flow is the $200. Player A would show a receipt of $200 and Player B would show an expenditure of $200 under investing activity in their respective Statements of Cash Flows. The underlying swap would not be shown but could have an impact on the Income Statement if either player needed to recognize a gain or loss on the transaction.

In preparing a Statement of Cash Flows, students may choose to use a worksheet or T-account approach. In either approach, the emphasis is on identifying and summarizing the cash flow impacts of the enterprise's transactions. Students are referred to their textbook for more detail and guidance.

REQUIREMENTS:

1. Prepare a Statement of Cash Flows (Indirect Method) for your company as of the end of the game.

2. Prepare a Statement of Cash Flows (Direct Method) for your company as of the end of the game.

3. Compare and contrast the results of operations as measured on an accrual basis (Income Statement) and a cash basis (Statement of Cash Flows). What are the advantages and disadvantages of each of the approaches to assessing the results of operations for a specific period of time?

ASSIGNMENT IV

BASIC FINANCIAL STATEMENT ANALYSIS

AN OVERVIEW OF FINANCIAL STATEMENT ANALYSIS

The financial statements of an enterprise contain a wealth of data, all of which helps the reader to evaluate the financial status and performance of the company. Unfortunately, there is often so much data presented that the reader may have a difficult time developing a coherent and integrated understanding about what has happened to the company being scrutinized. To assist in the evaluation process, accountants, auditors and readers of financial statements have developed a number of techniques for analyzing financial statements. The goal of this analysis is to derive a coherent understanding and evaluation of the company by examining important and logical relationships among the data presented in the statements.

Two general techniques are particularly useful for evaluating financial statements: common size financial statements and ratio analysis. **Common size financial statements** are prepared by transforming raw numbers in the financial statements into percentages by dividing each balance by a common base. The base for the Income Statement is typically total sales or total revenue. The base for the Balance Sheet is typically total assets. By transforming the raw data, the percentages can be analyzed for consistent trends either over time or between accounts. For example, this form of analysis highlights the relationship between expenses and revenues and the relative magnitude of the components of the balance sheet.

Ratio analysis involves comparing data from different parts of the financial statements that is logically related. Table IV-1 lists some of the best known and most frequently used ratios. In general, the ratios fall into five categories. (Not all of these ratios will be pertinent for your *MONOPOLY*® game company since many of the ratios were developed for analyzing a retailing or manufacturing company.)

> (1) Liquidity Ratios: These ratios provide an indication of the company's ability to meet their obligations in the short term.
>
> (2) Debt Management or Solvency Ratios: These ratios provide an indication of the company's ability to meet their obligations in the long term.
>
> (3) Asset Management Ratios: These ratios provide an indication of how efficient and effective the company is at managing the assets that they possess. In order to interpret these ratios, it is important to understand the basic nature of the enterprise's operations. These ratios would need to be modified in order to analyze the statements of your company.

(4) Profitability Ratios: These ratios provide an indication of how well the company is doing on an overall basis.

(5) Market Value Ratios: These ratios provide an indication of how well investors and potential investors think the company is doing. (These ratios are not meaningful in the present assignment).

This is not an exhaustive list of all possible ratios. Analysts often construct additional ratios given the unique circumstances of the company they are analyzing. Also, the computation of ratios may be subject to data limitations. For example, ratios which are based on "average" balances (e.g., turnover ratios) may be computed using year end balances rather than average annual balances because the data is more readily available. This is not wrong, but must be considered when interpreting the results.

Finally, students should be aware that the interpretation of ratios and common size statements is more of an art than a science. The significance of ratios or percentages must be interpreted in the context of what is known about a company. A specific ratio value may be critically important in one instance but not very meaningful in another. Ultimately, the objective of performing financial statement analysis is to obtain a better understanding of what has happened to an enterprise and why than is obtainable from the raw data presented in the financial statements. When you are done with your analysis, you should be able to tell the "story" of the enterprise in a concise and coherent manner. You should also be able to reach an overall conclusion about the company's performance which is fully supported by the facts as you understand them.

Table IV-2 contains an example of financial statement analysis for a typical manufacturing company. A few points should be noted about Table IV-2. First, the table presents both ratios and common size statements. These are complementary, not alternative, approaches to analysis. Second, three years of data is presented. This allows the reader to examine the company's performance over time. The more periods that you can analyze, the better the insight you can obtain. Unfortunately, you will only have one year's data when you analyze your own company. Third, industry data is presented. This data represents the results of a group of peer companies in the same industry as the company being analyzed. This comparison data is useful for determining how well the company is doing against its competition. You will be able to make this comparison for your company by comparing to other players.

REQUIREMENTS:

1. Prepare a common size Income Statement and Balance Sheet for your company as of the end of the game.

2. Compute the ratios described in Table IV-1 for your company. Note, some of the ratios will not be computable because your company doesn't have receivables or inventory. These ratios should be set equal to zero.

3. Prepare a brief analysis of the financial statements of your company using the common size financial statements and the ratios.

4. Which ratios are most meaningful for your analysis? Why? Which ratios are least meaningful for your analysis? Why?

5. How does your company compare to the other players in your group? Which player did the best and which player did the worst? Why? Who is the *winner* in your group? Use specific data (percentages or ratios) to support your choice.

6. Obtain the results for the *winner* in each of the other groups in the class. Which player is the *grand winner* for the entire class? Why? Use specific data and comparisons to support your choice.

TABLE IV-1

COMMON FINANCIAL STATEMENT RATIOS

Liquidity Ratios:

Quick Ratio

$$\frac{\text{Cash} + \text{Marketable securities} + \text{Net Receivables}}{\text{Current Liabilities}}$$

Current Ratio

$$\frac{\text{Current Assets}}{\text{Current Liabilities}}$$

Debt Management Ratios:

Payable Turnover

$$\frac{\text{Cost of Goods Sold}}{\text{Average Accounts Payable}}$$

Debt Ratio

$$\frac{\text{Total Liabilities}}{\text{Total Assets}}$$

Interest Coverage Ratio
(Times Interest Earned)

$$\frac{\text{Earnings before Interest \& Taxes}}{\text{Interest Expense}}$$

Asset Management Ratios:

Inventory Turnover

$$\frac{\text{Cost of Goods Sold}}{\text{Average Inventory}}$$

Receivable Turnover

$$\frac{\text{Net Sales or Revenue}}{\text{Average Net Receivables}}$$

Fixed Asset Turnover

$$\frac{\text{Net Sales or Revenue}}{\text{Average Net Fixed Assets}}$$

Total Asset Turnover

$$\frac{\text{Net Sales or Revenue}}{\text{Total Assets}}$$

Average Days to Collect

365/Receivable Turnover

Average Days to Sell

365/Inventory Turnover

Average Operating Cycle

Average Days to Sell + Average Days to Collect

Depreciation Rate

$$\frac{\text{Depreciation Expense}}{\text{Net Fixed Assets}}$$

TABLE IV-1 (Continued)

Profitability Ratios:

Return on Assets

$$\frac{\text{Net Income}}{\text{Total Assets}}$$

Return on Equity

$$\frac{\text{Net Income - Preferred Stock Dividends}}{\text{Total Common Equity}}$$

Profit Margin

$$\frac{\text{Net Income}}{\text{Net Sales}}$$

Earnings Power

$$\frac{\text{Earnings before Interest \& Taxes}}{\text{Total Assets}}$$

Market Value Ratios:

Price/Earnings

$$\frac{\text{Common Stock Price}}{\text{Earnings per Share}}$$

Earnings per Share

$$\frac{\text{Net Income for the Current Period}}{\text{Number of Common Stock Shares}}$$

Market/Book

$$\frac{\text{Common Stock Share Price}}{\text{Common Stock Book Value}}$$

Dividend Payout

$$\frac{\text{Dividends paid out}}{\text{Net Income}}$$

Book value per share

$$\frac{\text{Total Equity attributable to Common Stock}}{\text{Number of Common Stock Shares}}$$

TABLE IV-2

AN EXAMPLE OF FINANCIAL STATEMENT ANALYSIS

| | | | | Common Size Financial Statements | | | |
INCOME STATEMENTS	1991	1992	1993	1991	1992	1993	Industry average
Net Sales	$702.00	$760.00	$800.00	100.00%	100.00%	100.00%	100.00%
Cost of goods sold excl deprn	(430.00)	(465.00)	(495.00)	-61.25%	-61.18%	-61.88%	-62.52%
Depreciation	(30.00)	(35.00)	(40.00)	-4.27%	-4.61%	-5.00%	-4.26%
Gross profit	242.00	260.00	265.00	34.47%	34.21%	33.13%	33.22%
Admin. & Selling expense	(65.00)	(68.00)	(70.00)	-9.26%	-8.95%	-8.75%	-9.56%
Other expenses	(60.00)	(65.00)	(65.00)	-8.55%	-8.55%	-8.13%	-9.16%
EBIT	117.00	127.00	130.00	16.67%	16.71%	16.25%	14.50%
Interest: short-term loans	(0.67)	(0.70)	(0.64)	-0.10%	-0.09%	-0.08%	-1.29%
Interest: long-term loans	(4.60)	(4.60)	(4.60)	-0.66%	-0.61%	-0.58%	-1.14%
Interest income	1.01	1.06	1.12	0.14%	0.14%	0.14%	0.43%
Net Income before taxes	112.74	122.76	125.88	16.06%	16.15%	15.74%	12.50%
Income taxes	(45.10)	(49.10)	(50.35)	-6.42%	-6.46%	-6.29%	-4.44%
Net income after taxes	67.64	73.66	75.53	9.64%	9.69%	9.44%	8.06%
Dividends	(28.31)	(32.01)	(33.00)	-4.03%	-4.21%	-4.13%	-4.03%
To retained earnings	39.33	41.65	42.53	5.60%	5.48%	5.32%	4.03%
Number of shares (000)	60.00	60.00	60.00				
Earnings per share	1.13	1.23	1.26				
Dividends per share	0.47	0.53	0.55				
Price per share	11.25	12.27	13.60				
Book value per share	8.25	8.94	9.65				
Net Cash Flow			1.54				

NOTE: This illustration is taken from "Financial Accounting with Lotus 1-2-3: Text and Models" by Eugene F. Brigham and W. Robert Knechel (San Diego: Harcourt Brace Jovanovich, 1990), pp. 244, 245 and 247.

TABLE IV-2 (Continued)

AN EXAMPLE OF FINANCIAL STATEMENT ANALYSIS

				Common Size Financial Statements			
BALANCE SHEETS	1991	1992	1993	1991	1992	1993	Industry average
Cash	$6.22	$6.46	$8.00	1.00%	0.97%	1.13%	1.73%
Marketable Securities	8.36	13.01	16.00	1.35%	1.96%	2.27%	3.16%
Accounts Receivable	144.00	175.00	195.00	23.26%	26.34%	27.66%	25.93%
Inventory	182.39	210.00	221.00	29.47%	31.60%	31.35%	30.82%
Current Assets	340.97	404.47	440.00	55.09%	60.87%	62.41%	61.64%
Plant, property & equipment	357.00	375.00	420.00	57.68%	56.44%	59.57%	
Allowance for depreciation	(79.00)	(115.00)	(155.00)	-12.76%	-17.31%	-21.99%	
Net long-term assets	278.00	260.00	265.00	44.91%	39.13%	37.59%	38.36%
Total Assets	$618.97	$664.47	$705.00	100.00%	100.00%	100.00%	100.00%
Accounts Payable	$43.00	$45.00	$40.00	6.95%	6.77%	5.67%	6.29%
Notes payable	6.65	7.00	8.00	1.07%	1.05%	1.13%	19.37%
Accruals	28.50	30.00	32.00	4.60%	4.51%	4.54%	5.16%
Current liabilities	78.15	82.00	80.00	12.63%	12.34%	11.35%	30.82%
Mortgage bonds	46.00	46.00	46.00	7.43%	6.92%	6.52%	19.18%
Long-term debt	46.00	46.00	46.00	7.43%	6.92%	6.52%	19.18%
Total liabilities	124.15	128.00	126.00	20.06%	19.26%	17.87%	50.00%
Common stock	445.00	445.00	445.00	71.89%	66.97%	63.12%	31.26%
Retained earnings	49.82	91.47	133.99	8.05%	13.77%	19.01%	18.74%
Total equity	494.82	536.47	578.99	79.94%	80.74%	82.13%	50.00%
Total liabilities & equity	$618.97	$664.47	$704.99	100.00%	100.00%	100.00%	100.00%

TABLE IV-2 (Continued)

AN EXAMPLE OF FINANCIAL STATEMENT ANALYSIS

RATIO ANALYSIS	1991	1992	1993	Industry average
Liquidity Ratios:				
Quick	2.03	2.37	2.74	1.00
Current	4.36	4.93	5.50	2.00
Asset Management Ratios:				
Inventory Turnover*	2.36	2.21	2.24	2.03
Receivable Turnover*	4.88	4.34	4.10	4.56
Long-term Asset Turnover*	2.53	2.92	3.02	3.15
Total Asset Turnover*	1.13	1.14	1.13	0.90
Average days to collect	74.87	84.05	88.97	80.00
Average days to sell	154.82	164.84	162.96	180.00
Average operating cycle	229.69	248.88	251.93	260.00
Depreciation/fixed assets	0.08	0.09	0.10	0.11
Debt Management Ratios:				
Payable Turnover*	10.00	10.33	12.38	11.00
Debt Ratio	20.06%	19.26%	17.87%	50.00%
Times Interest Earned	27.46	29.95	31.55	7.25
Profitability Ratios:				
Return on Assets	10.93%	11.08%	10.71%	7.25%
Return on Equity	13.67%	13.73%	13.04%	14.50%
Profit Margin	9.64%	9.69%	9.44%	8.06%
Earning Power	18.90%	19.11%	18.44%	20.00%
Market Value Ratios:				
Price/Earnings	9.98	10.00	10.80	10.00
Market/Book	1.36	1.37	1.41	1.60
Other Ratios:				
Dividend/Share	0.47	0.53	0.55	
Earnings/Share	1.13	1.23	1.26	
Dividend Payout	41.85%	43.46%	43.69%	50.00%

*   These ratios were computed using year-end balances in
     the denominator.

Working Papers

JOURNALS, LEDGERS AND WORKSHEETS

The following worksheets, journal and ledgers have been included in this package for your use. Some of the column headings have been completed for you as a guide to the usage of the schedules.

Form	Number of Copies	Page
Chart of Accounts (suggested)	1	40
General Journal	12	41
General Ledger, Partial headings	36	53
Cash Receipts Journal, Headings complete	2	89
Cash Receipts Journal, No headings	4	91
Cash Disbursements Journal, Headings complete	2	95
Cash Disbursements Journal, No headings	4	97
2-column worksheets, blank	8	101
3-column worksheets, blank	8	109
4-column worksheets, blank	6	117
7-column worksheets, blank	4	123
Long-term Assets Ledger pages	6	127
Notes Payable Ledger pages	2	133
10 column worksheets, blank	4	135

CHART OF ACCOUNTS

<u>Balance Sheet:</u>
100	Cash
110	Receivables
200	Land
210	Investments--Railroads
220	Investments--Utilities
250	Buildings--Houses
251	Accumulated Depreciation--Houses
260	Buildings--Hotels
261	Accumulated Depreciation--Hotels
270	Other Assets
300	Mortgage Payable
310	Interest Payable
320	Income Taxes Payable
330	Other Payables
400	Contributed Capital
410	Retained Earnings
420	Prepaid Rent

<u>Income Statement:</u>
500	Rent Revenue
510	Consulting Revenue
520	Investment Income (use for utilities and railroads)
530	Interest Revenue
540	Miscellaneous Revenue
600	Rent Expense
610	Property Tax Expense
620	Income Tax Expense
630	Fines and Penalties Expense
640	Repairs and Maintenance Expense
650	Interest Expense
660	Depreciation Expense
670	Miscellaneous Expenses
700	Gains on Disposal of Property
710	Losses on Disposal of Property
720	Other Gains and Losses
601	Prepaid Rent

NOTE: Students should feel free to add accounts to this list as they deem necessary. Be sure to note the account number and title for any new accounts.

Name _____

Section _____

GENERAL JOURNAL

Page _____

Date	Account Titles and Explanations	PR	Debit	Credit

45

GENERAL JOURNAL

Date	Account Titles and Explanations	PR	Debit	Credit

Name _____

Section _____

GENERAL JOURNAL

Page _____

Date	Account Titles and Explanations	PR	Debit	Credit

Name _____

Section _____

GENERAL JOURNAL

Page _____

Date	Account Titles and Explanations	PR	Debit	Credit

48

Name _____

Section _____

GENERAL JOURNAL

Page _____

Date	Account Titles and Explanations	PR	Debit	Credit

Name _____

Section _____

GENERAL JOURNAL

Page _____

Date	Account Titles and Explanations	PR	Debit	Credit

Name _____

Section _____

GENERAL JOURNAL

Page _____

Date		Account Titles and Explanations	PR	Debit	Credit

51

Name _____

Section _____

GENERAL JOURNAL

Page _____

Date	Account Titles and Explanations	PR	Debit	Credit

52

Copyright © 1992 by Harcourt Brace Jovanovich, Inc. All rights reserved.

Name _____

Section _____

GENERAL LEDGER

ACCOUNT: Acct. No. _____

Date	Transactions	PR	Debit	Credit	Balance

71

Name _____

Section _____

GENERAL LEDGER

ACCOUNT: Acct. No. _____

Date	Transactions	PR	Debit	Credit	Balance

72

Name _____

Section _____

GENERAL LEDGER

ACCOUNT: \qquad\qquad Acct. No. _____

Date	Transactions	PR	Debit	Credit	Balance

Name _____

Section _____

GENERAL LEDGER

ACCOUNT:

Acct. No. _____

Date	Transactions	PR	Debit	Credit	Balance

Name _____

Section _____

GENERAL LEDGER

ACCOUNT: Acct. No. _____

Date	Transactions	PR	Debit	Credit	Balance

Name _____

Section _____

GENERAL LEDGER

ACCOUNT:

Acct. No. _____

Date	Transactions	PR	Debit	Credit	Balance

76

Name _____

Section _____

GENERAL LEDGER

ACCOUNT: _____   Acct. No. _____

Date	Transactions	PR	Debit	Credit	Balance

Name _____

Section _____

GENERAL LEDGER

ACCOUNT:

Acct. No. _____

Date	Transactions	PR	Debit	Credit	Balance

Name _____

Section _____

GENERAL LEDGER

ACCOUNT: Acct. No. _____

Date	Transactions	PR	Debit	Credit	Balance

Name _____

Section _____

GENERAL LEDGER

ACCOUNT: _____   Acct. No. _____

Date		Transactions	PR	Debit	Credit	Balance

80

Name _____

Section _____

GENERAL LEDGER

ACCOUNT: Acct. No. _____

Date	Transactions	PR	Debit	Credit	Balance

Name _____

Section _____

GENERAL LEDGER

ACCOUNT: _____   Acct. No. _____

Date	Transactions	PR	Debit	Credit	Balance

82

Name _____

Section _____

GENERAL LEDGER

ACCOUNT: _____   Acct. No. _____

Date	Transactions	PR	Debit	Credit	Balance

GENERAL LEDGER

ACCOUNT: Acct. No. _____

Date	Transactions	PR	Debit	Credit	Balance

Name _____

Section _____

GENERAL LEDGER

ACCOUNT: Acct. No. _____

Date	Transactions	PR	Debit	Credit	Balance

85

Name _____

Section _____

GENERAL LEDGER

ACCOUNT: _____   Acct. No. _____

Date	Transactions	PR	Debit	Credit	Balance

Name _____

Section _____

GENERAL LEDGER

ACCOUNT: Acct. No. _____

Date	Transactions	PR	Debit	Credit	Balance

GENERAL LEDGER

ACCOUNT:

Date	Transactions	PR	Debit	Credit	Balance

CASH RECEIPTS JOURNAL

Date	Notes	Debit Cash	Credit Rent Revenue	Credit Salary	Other Accounts	Credit Amount

CASH RECEIPTS JOURNAL

Date	Notes	Debit Cash	Credit Rent Revenue	Credit Salary	Other Accounts	Credit Amount

CASH RECEIPTS JOURNAL

Name

Section

91

Name

Section

92

CASH RECEIPTS JOURNAL

Name _____

Section _____

CASH RECEIPTS JOURNAL

Name

Section

CASH DISBURSEMENTS JOURNAL

Date	Notes	Credit Cash	Debit Rent Expense	Debit Property	Other Accounts	Debit Amount

CASH DISBURSEMENTS JOURNAL

Date	Notes	Credit Cash	Debit Rent Expense	Debit Property	Other Accounts	Debit Amount

96

Name

Section

97

Name

Section

Name

Section

99

CASH DISBURSEMENTS JOURNAL

Name _____

Section _____

100

Name _____

Section _____

Name _____

Section _____

103

Name _____

Section _____

105

Name _____

Section _____

Name _____

Section _____

107

Name _____

Section _____

108

109

Name _____

Section _____

Name _____

Section _____

112

113

Name _____

Section _____

114

Name _____

Section _____

116

Name _____

Section _____

Name _____

Section _____

118

Name _____

Section _____

Name _____

Section _____

Name _____

Section _____

Name _____

Section _____

Name _____

Section _____

Name _____

Section _____

Name _____

Section _____

125

Name _____

Section _____

126

Name _____

Section _____

LONG-TERM ASSETS LEDGER

Asset Description	Type? Land/ House	Date (Turn) Bought	Price Paid	Expected Life	Annual Depreciation Expense	Depreciation Expense: Current	Date (Turn) Sold	Selling Price	Gain or (Loss)

127

LONG-TERM ASSETS LEDGER

Asset Description	Type? Land/ House	Date (Turn) Bought	Price Paid	Expected Life	Annual Depreciation Expense	Depreciation Expense: Current	Date (Turn) Sold	Selling Price	Gain or (Loss)

128

LONG-TERM ASSETS LEDGER

Asset Description	Type? Land/ House	Date (Turn) Bought	Price Paid	Expected Life	Annual Depreciation Expense	Depreciation Expense: Current	Date (Turn) Sold	Selling Price	Gain or (Loss)

129

LONG-TERM ASSETS LEDGER

Asset Description	Type? Land/ House	Date (Turn) Bought	Price Paid	Expected Life	Annual Depreciation Expense	Depreciation Expense: Current	Date (Turn) Sold	Selling Price	Gain or (Loss)

130

Name _____

Section _____

LONG-TERM ASSETS LEDGER

Asset Description	Type? Land/ House	Date (Turn) Bought	Price Paid	Expected Life	Annual Depreciation Expense	Depreciation Expense: Current	Date (Turn) Sold	Selling Price	Gain or (Loss)

131

Name _____

Section _____

LONG-TERM ASSETS LEDGER

Asset Description	Type? Land/ House	Date (Turn) Bought	Price Paid	Expected Life	Annual Depreciation Expense	Depreciation Expense: Current	Date (Turn) Sold	Selling Price	Gain or (Loss)

132

NOTES PAYABLE LEDGER

Property Mortgaged (or other description)	Date (Turn) of Loan	Amount Borrowed	Date (Turn) Repaid	Total Amount Repaid	Interest Paid	Year-End Interest Accrual

133

NOTES PAYABLE LEDGER

Name _____

Section _____

Property Mortgaged (or other description)	Date (Turn) of Loan	Amount Borrowed	Date (Turn) Repaid	Total Amount Repaid	Interest Paid	Year-End Interest Accrual

134